MW01089996

THE MLK IMAGE: THE SAFE BLACK MALE

Raising Kids in a Divided Society

Dr. Kimberly N. Jackson

Library of Congress Control Number: 2020901983
ISBN 978-0-578-58009-8

I dedicate this book to all the blood, sweat, and tears of my parents and grandparents over the years that have allowed me the freedom to be me.

Contents

Acknowledgments

WOULD LIKE TO EXPRESS SINCERE GRATITUDE TO A NUMBER OF people who assisted in bringing this work to completion. My father, Steve Jackson, and my son, Jacob Jackson, are the two who inspired my thinking, and it is important to me that they know the depth of the love that my heart has for both of them. I would also like to thank my mother, Rachel Jackson-Bowens, for listening to multiple reads as the book was being developed. I have a number of friends who supported my efforts through their early encouragement: Anissa Burdett, Adriana Ochoa, and Dr. Alison Reeves. They helped me gain the confidence to actually share my work with the world; their early validation helped me to confidently keep moving forward. Ms. Burdett was also the driving force in moving this work to publication, and I cannot thank her enough for helping me through the process.

I would like to show gratitude to Susan Lybarger (Aunt Susan) for taking the time to both read and discuss this work with me from her perspective. Our world is a fragile place right now, and it is critical that we find ways to unify our efforts toward a better existence for all of our kids. I wanted to ensure that this book was readable by all, and I am grateful to Aunt Susan for going down that path with me. Her honesty and validation that the ability of the words to cross barriers of beliefs and experiences fulfilled a foundational goal of the writing from the beginning. The discoveries that she opened my mind up to helped me realize that the work was broader than my initial audience. We exist in a very difficult time politically and socially, and the more people open their minds to understand those around them with a greater willingness to use that understanding as a bridge, the sooner our world will begin to heal. Thank you, Aunt Susan, for connecting hands with me as part of that bridge.

Last but definitely not least, I would like to thank God for the circumstances of my life that led me down this path. I am eternally grateful for His grace, mercy, and love that He has shown toward me throughout my life and for trusting me with this Word. I am grateful for the transitional role that He has placed me in, and I embrace that role to the fullest in all that I write. His desire is that we feel His love by discovering who He intended us to be, and living and fulfilling that purpose to our fullest. On that individual path of discovery is where we meet, understand, and learn to love our true self. Embrace the things that energize you, face the things that scare you, challenge any perceived limitations; it is in those places and those experiences that we discover our purpose and truly begin to uncover all the beauty and ability within ourselves.

Preface

WHEN I STARTED WRITING THIS BOOK, MY GOAL WAS TO share the discoveries that I made while attempting to "successfully" raise black boys in our current society. But as I delved deeper into my topic, I realized that my purpose was broader, and that my discoveries could apply more globally to raising children in today's society. Knowing this, I have broadened the scope of this book, but I will still explore these dynamics as they relate to the black male.

It would be narrow-minded to only speak about the struggle of raising black boys and not acknowledge the larger struggle of raising kids in a world that feels very foreign to many of us. New concerns, some may call epidemics, surface so frequently that it is difficult to know whether we are responsibly keeping up as parents until we face a crisis, or our child has become an independent adult. As an educator, I struggle daily with trying to figure out how to interact with and reach young people. The older I get, the further removed I feel from the lingo, popular trends, and struggles that make up their reality. Current issues and tragedies such as suicides, which are on the rise, force a growing number of children and families to make education and other self-improvement practices take a back seat. Although parents focus on helping their children to develop and become good people and upstanding citizens, sometimes just keeping their child(ren) alive is their first and foremost priority. Even in situations where a crisis does not cause immediate life or death, many issues such as those related to drugs and sex can shake even the calmest parent, especially in the age of social media and electronics.

As I write this book, I am overwhelmed by the number of issues that I have seen young people face just from my experiences within the school environment. At times, it feels as though the "world" is creatively finding new ways to harm or even kill them. Sometimes their own poor choices create these harmful elements, and at other times our bad choices and other external factors regarding the world we will leave them create a harmful environment that they must face. I have often thought that my coworkers and I should host a reality show within the school because most people would not believe the "reality" that kids are now having to deal with. Is the world just that much more dangerous than it was before, or are our kids more susceptible to negative influences? Have our youth become that misguided? Are they soft?

Background

ALTHOUGH I BELIEVE THE WORLD HAS CHANGED IMMENSELY since our parents' youthful days, I do not believe that this poses our ultimate or largest problem. Clearly the variables that cause parents to struggle in the process of raising kids are numerous, but they cannot be attributed solely to one factor because life is overwhelmingly complex. I believe, instead, that some elements attribute more than others, depending on each family's and child's experiences and situations. I am not dismissing worldly factors and their impact on our current struggles in guiding our kids, but I do, however, feel that these worldly elements take a back seat to a much larger issue: un/misinformed and antiquated parenting. Many parents, even me, continue to rely on paper map guidance to direct our kids in a GPS-paced world. Yes, I just said that we as parents, and the methods that we use to parent, are the biggest barriers to our children's success. Stay with me, though, because if ineffective parenting is the biggest barrier, then effective parenting is the biggest factor that can help promote success.

And when it comes to black males, the struggle is even heightened. If you don't believe me, then just look at the declining success of black males born in two-parent, middle-class homes. Compare that to the disparities in the achievement levels between black males and black females, and you will notice that this is a major issue. I want to give special attention to the struggle of black parents because we seem to have an especially hard time helping our male children find their path and staying on it. Later I will discuss how history and education have guided blacks and how this impacts how we have parented our children over the years.

Although blacks have gained opportunities and greater economic status, a belief system built on a foundation of fear with a focus on the attainment of safety and security continues to fuel our expectations about how our children should behave. Early on, parents had strict views about behavior, very rigid expectations of what kids should do, especially in public. Parents wanted their children to be safe first and foremost, and they also wanted their kids accepted by the community. For generations, parents have raised black children with strict yet inconsistent guidelines, along with strong physical punishments based on historical influences, which include an underlying religious element that teaches if you "spare the rod, you spoil the child." The interpretation of "the rod" for many, not just blacks, can range from a literal interpretation of a physical rod indicating physical punishment, all the way to a more abstract understanding of the rod as a symbol of correction. Historically, black families have taken a more literal interpretation of this parenting responsibility; therefore, parental guidance has focused more on discipline and correction rather than discovery and individuality. Many families believe that the right path toward success leads to a quality nine-to-five job with a great pension, and many older blacks believe that if their children follow that same path they will see the same successes and outcomes. But over time that path can strip away many of the motivators that helped push and drive our children to stay the course. In turn, our children have realized that the successes found by following this route are less glamorous than in the past.

I am not criticizing the success that these methods have had, and at times continue to help people rise above their circumstances. But, as many of our children now enter this world in a different place than we did or truly understand their freedoms and opportunities, we have to both see and acknowledge that the ways of the past are not effective for guiding the youth of today. Older blacks, especially, continue to adhere to these beliefs almost as though each choice and action is taken directly from the Bible with truth and certainty, yet they fail to recognize the decreasing number of successes. This alienates the younger generation, creating a deeper and deeper divide between two groups that truly need each other for survival. Parents of black males, especially, desperately need a change in thinking and methodology to set our kids up for success.

Just because I took a moment to provide specifics related to my race does not mean that this dynamic does not exist for others. Within my role in the school system, I have seen parents of all types struggling with this very same issue. The truth of the matter is that parents, in general, often feel they are parenting blindly. Regardless of feelings or reason, the end result is a desperate need for change. We have not kept up with what our children need to meet the demands of the world for which we are preparing them. We are still preparing our children for the world based on the practices and goals from our own upbringing. Overall, we still adhere to thinking based on the world that we were being prepared for, not the current world as it actually exists for them or the future. We have become so conditioned to rely on what has worked in the past that we fail to discover what works in the present. We are so busy doing this that planning and even considering what may work in the future is not even on the radar. That is a lot to handle and may feel like a bit of a kick in the gut, so let me explain where I am coming from.

We have embarked on a new day where the economic divide seems to be growing. Youth on the poverty end of the spectrum are experiencing more and more trauma while the youth on the more affluent end are engaging in higher levels of self-discovery and self-actualization. For those struggling, how to survive has changed very little over time, but it has become more violent and more dangerous with fewer clear paths to safety. Poverty has become a culture within itself that engulfs families for generations; there are many families and young people for which poverty and struggle is all they have ever known, and this is not exclusive to any race or group. Without motivation and either guidance, luck, or a bit of both, it is very difficult to find the path out of poverty. We all hear stories about those who "make it out," and the media continues to focus on those special feel-good stories, but they have yet to become the norm in the reality show of life.

When we discuss the struggles young people living in poverty have in finding success, we have to look at the lack of resources and support that exist for these individuals that impedes them from reaching the mark. Many do not even know that the mark exists because they have very little vision outside of their daily struggles. Without vision, it is difficult to find purpose. Without purpose, it is difficult to identify direction, which is what I describe as a literal *Birdbox* existence. This leaves many young people who grow up in high-poverty areas without the ability to extend their goals beyond those things that are glamorized within their environment because they lack the exposure to other options. Poor schools, lack of consistent and adequate housing, lack of basic resources, and lack of diversity within the community and schools leaves many young people from these poverty-stricken areas completely unprepared. Without the skills, behaviors, and self-confidence to approach a more economically stable existence, they cannot take advantage of any of the opportunities that may come their way. Although these social dynamics are important and we desperately need to address them, they are vast and a topic for another book. The purpose here is to simply describe the conditions that exist.

Young people who have minimal experience struggling economically have a completely different story and obstacle. They do not typically spend time thinking about their basic needs or safety. For the average young person in this situation, they are not preoccupied with worrying about such basic needs. For these young people, their parents or guardians take care of their basic needs and safety, which allows them the luxury to focus on other areas—themselves and their own happiness. This is a shift from the days of conformity to a period of self-fulfillment and self-actualization. This change in focus falls predictably in line with the various stages discussed by Abraham Maslow, one of our world's greatest authorities on motivation. But, how did we get here?

At some point before or during my generation's childhood (60s, 70s, 80s), American society adopted a more politically correct focus that placed a greater importance on the global good. This focus placed family, country, and religion in a coexistent role with equity and equality for all. For many, their religious convictions and beliefs were the foundation for these fights and struggles, and this is where our parents' parents spread their wings of self-advocacy and discovery. Many of our grandparents had jobs that afforded our parents more options, and they placed a greater importance on education, especially for minorities attempting to move up the economic ladder. For the black community, specifically, the fight for civil rights was the outlet, and it originated and took place within the context of the church and religion. The black church was everything rolled up into one for the movement, and due to its role, the church's strength and reputation increased, establishing it as the hub for the successful black family. The civil rights movement gave power and prestige to the black church, but the success of that movement, along with the freedoms and recognitions gained in other fights, created a greater divide between church and state. Tax laws required nonprofit entities to take a hands-off approach to politics, and the black church lost its overall place in the societal fight to influence black people's growth and progress. Just like that, the movement virtually eliminated the role of the black church in black people's civil issues.

The generations that followed began raising their children, irrelevant of race, with a different focus and less emphasis on the elements of the past. The younger generations gained a reputation of lacking commitment and work ethic with no focus, while they viewed the older generations as stagnant, narrow-minded, and judgmental. Later in this book I will go into more detail about why I believe this dynamic has occurred based on Maslow's hierarchy of needs—the famous triangle that describes what motivates each of us based on the focus of our attention. This theory, in my opinion, helps to explain our current problems and gives us a hint toward a solution.

The connection of this theory to real life as it pertains to this book's topic is the financial success that many of our parents, and those of my generation, have seen. This success has allowed us to shield our children from the majority of struggles or even uncomfortable moments that we faced growing up. This success, however, requires us to adopt a new way of motivating and reaching our children, plain and simple. Such basic needs as food, water, and shelter will likely never motivate young people whose parents experienced such success. This means that those motivators that drove many of our parents and us, at least indirectly, do not exist for many of these children and, therefore, do not work. This is especially true for children who have always had financial stability. Knowing this allows us to begin to look for solutions—a different or new way that incorporates appropriate and relevant practices from the past along with new, individualized discoveries that customize each child's upbringing to truly focus on what is in their best interest for long-term success, fulfillment, and happiness.

As I have learned about what motivates my kids, all of which have lived through different times and conditions within my life, I have begun to understand that there is a different way of managing young people and guiding them than what I experienced and have so often seen. In reality, it is not a different or new way at all but rather applying old knowledge that we have found useful, and using that knowledge to enhance how we interact with our kids in today's world. We should focus on helping our children discover who they are, not based on what will impress the neighbor or what salary or wage we desire for them, but rather based on what they like, prefer, and do best. We should help them discover what provides them fulfillment in life and what makes them happy, not based on our needs and desires, but based on theirs. At times, this may mean exposing them to or participating in things we do not like to ensure that they can make their own decisions. This may mean that you may need to support their choice to pursue a vocational-based path in spite of a strong family history of earning four-year college degrees.

It is vital that we discover our children's strengths, weaknesses, and preferences to help them in their self-discoveries and guide them toward their best future. Often we feel we know what the best future and life is for our children. We know what we want for them and we have a path in our minds of how they can best get there. Even the most open-minded parent wants the best for their child, whatever that means to them. The issue is when our hopes, dreams, and visions of a future for our children intertwines with their gifts, talents, and interests. Unfortunately, our hopes and dreams often have a greater voice and power over the outcome. I am not saying that parental influence on the future of our kids is bad. What I am proposing is that as parents we should focus our attention and time on discovery and try to understand who our kids are outside of who we want them to be, and use that knowledge to help guide them toward who they were intended to be. There are so many things that we can learn about each of our children, we just have to take the time to do it.

At some point in history, society gave more prestige to certain professions than others. The truth is we are still in that time. This perception of prestige motivated young people to go into careers based on factors that had very little to do with what they were best at or what they were interested in. Many raised to think this way chose their path based on expectations and image. Some that fell into this pattern were lucky enough to land in careers that were at least somewhat within the scope of their interests and gifts, but many have found themselves unhappy, exploring career changes at a later point in life that emphasize fulfillment and happiness rather than position, image, or prestige. The number of career changes that the average adult experiences in their lifetime—often up to seven—supports this dynamic. Some will argue this point, but I argue that many, if not most, people chose a profession before they have had time or opportunity to explore life enough to discover what they were good at or their interests outside of what their parents exposed them to. This is not putting down parents' efforts, but a reality of the times and a societal trend.

The group raised under these conditions, which I call the *economic bridge generation*, was afforded travel and extra opportunities. Many of this group's parents did their best to provide a better life for their children than what they had growing up, and, overall, they were extremely successful at doing that. For many of these parents, however, their work ethic was a result of their experiences growing up where they may have struggled or had to put their family's needs ahead of their own. The economic bridge generation learned directly from them, but now, in a watered-down version, their kids are learning from them—a group of people who only experienced many of their parents' struggles secondhand through their stories or interactions with their grandparents. Many within this group are not necessarily in their ideal careers or paths, yet they are comfortable, which has shielded their children from the struggles that their parents tried to shield them from, sometimes even greater. The children in this economic bridge generation are not, however, finding the same success, especially black males. This hits home for me because I am a representative of this economic bridge group and I am facing the challenging task of assisting my sons in finding their path. More and more of our children are falling short of the "do better than your parents" standard, often falling back to financial levels not seen for generations within the family. What does this mean and how do we regain the positive momentum? With our understanding of our kids growing daily—their strengths, needs, and interests—how do we utilize that information to help guide them as our parents did for us? How do we guide our children toward a better life by helping them find fulfillment in living their best life and becoming their very best self?

As I relay what I feel are best practice methods and thinking toward raising children, some may feel defensive based on the differences in how they were raised and taught or how they have raised their own children. Some people may already feel offended based on what they read in the Preface and Background sections. In no way am I diminishing or disrespecting the efforts and sacrifices of our elders or any persons who have done their best. Rather, I respect their purpose, which allows me to discover my role and the role of the next generation in moving it forward. I challenge you to go beyond your "feelings" and begin to focus on what is best for each and every one of our children. It is my goal to stimulate thoughts and ideas that will increase the success and happiness of all of our children long-term. I challenge my own thinking as I challenge yours with our common purpose to give our kids the very best of our efforts, even if we are still discovering what that means.

I go back to my inspiration for writing this book, which is sheer reverence and respect to those who have allowed me the comfort and freedom to even think this way in conjunction with my responsibility to help my sons. Although I had taken on the parenting role with the older two boys, I had never done it at such a young and vulnerable stage as with the youngest. With his older brothers, I was given the privilege of finishing, fine-tuning, and fixing my parenting skills; for the sake of the pattern I will add failing. I do not claim success in any choices made with them because as adults now, their success is not based on my measure, but rather their own. How they feel about the quality of their lives is sheerly based on their opinion and feelings, not mine—they are not required to live by my gauge of success. I have learned to allow them the freedom to explore and discover their own paths with my unconditional love. I do not have to agree, I simply have to love them.

For some people, especially those who adhere to a belief system that maintains expectations for how others live their lives, this is very difficult. I have, however, learned that it is the easiest and best form of love to give to another, the freedom and acceptance to be themselves. For the older two as adults, it is very easy for me to take that type of hands-off approach, offering advice when they request it and my love and acceptance at all times because they are ultimately old enough to be responsible for their own choices and outcomes. This is not so easy, however, when faced with raising a child from the very begin-ning of their life. When my youngest son came into my care, for the first time, I was faced with molding my own raw clay—responsible for creating a solid foundation. When I realized the true magnitude of the responsibility to care for a child from birth until death do us part, I realized how critical every decision is since there are no redos or do-overs. I was faced with the reality that I really needed to consider my actions on a more serious level than anything I had in the past.

I realized that I needed to do this not based on a blind faith in what has always been or what I learned, but through my own research.

When I reached this point of enlightenment and I began looking into the plight and condition of young people being raised in our current times, I was forced to see that the ways of the past were not working very well for the kids of today. This put me at odds with just about every foundation and teaching that had been reinforced within me throughout my life. This put me at odds with just about all the critical people and places that I had grown to trust. Specifically, as I have matured and made the difficult transition between childhood and adulthood within my relationship with my parents, a complicated maneuver unfolded that no book, teacher, or grandmother's wisdom could have ever prepared me, or them, for. As I attempted to raise my youngest son and reconcile the beliefs from my upbringing with those of my adult life, I discovered that there is a mold that is expected of all of us. This mold of expectations existed for me as a parent—to follow the footsteps and beliefs of the family. These expectations often include the activities that we choose for our children as well as the places we expose them to. As a new parent to a baby, I felt a pressure that I had not felt before due to being blind to the dynamic. Prior to this point, I was more or less living in compliance. My awareness of this somewhat passive, yet aggressive expectation that exists for each of us started me on a search to understand what these expectations are for various groups and how they impact the lives of those adhering to these expectations, especially for my son as a male, and a black one specifically.

For some, they can barely feel the expectations, but for others these expectations dictate their acceptance and image in society, often within their family as well. These expectations create labels of right and wrong where the simplicity of difference should apply. As I considered the impact of this image, I realized that I needed to help my son have the courage and freedom to be his best self, whatever that means and however that unfolds, not based on anyone else's standards but his own. This is critical for happiness, but to achieve that, parents have to get their kids off to a good start and build a solid foundation of confidence. So much happens before our children are in a position to make their own choices. By the time they reach a point where they can, too often they are already off the path that would best fit them, and some never find their way back.

But black males are not the only ones burdened by the restrictions imposed on them due to an expected image. Historically, society also expects women to fill certain roles. Although current society has seen a significant reduction in some of these expectations, depending on your circumstances, many of them still exist. A perfect example are the roles and expectations related to raising kids and household activities such as cooking and cleaning. Again, we have come an extremely long way, but some parts of society still view these activities as women's work. This is also true in fashion, and how women dress. Women are often expected to dress a certain way, and if they don't, their wholesomeness or morality is questioned. Society as a whole still looks down on women who are considered to be more worldly or fast-paced. Women who wear something more revealing or just the opposite, more "masculine," endure judgment and ridicule. Society labels women who reveal too much as loose in their sexuality, while women who make more conservative clothing choices are "unapproachable" and "anti-male." Although we have made progress in how we judge people, these types of generalizations and judgments are still very prevalent. The expected image for women includes such characters as June Cleaver or Claire Huxtable, giving parameters for how a woman is to look and act to be considered a proper lady. Unfortunately, young girls grow up with these images, burning them into their minds and hearts, which creates restrictions in what they envision for themselves and what they might want to pursue. Women have fought these battles throughout the ages with many continuing the fight.

Although the examples of expectations regarding women have been around for ages, I feel that the expectations of black males have the greatest negative impact on the target group. For the black male, I call this box of expectations the MLK Image, based on the clean-cut, nonthreatening image of Dr. King. Although this is not a literal expectation, society judges the black male based on deviations from this image. The further black males veer from the MLK Image, the more likely society will see them as dangerous and less intelligent. To better understand the MLK Image, I will tell you a little about my life and the experiences that have shown me how the MLK Image perseveres in today's society. An understanding of this dynamic allows us to show respect toward our elders while also reconciling the differences that have reinforced the divide for too long.

It starts here. When I began writing this book in 2018, I had been a preacher's kid (PK) for 40 years. My dad has been a pastor for the same church for all but three years of my life. The church is a part of my family, it is a part of my culture, it is a way of life. Maybe in another book or at another time I will explore these dynamics at a deeper level, but for the purpose of this book, I want you to know that the church, family, and daily life were so intertwined that it was difficult to distinguish one from another. But that is how it was, and everyone just accepted it. Throughout the majority of my adult life, the expectations and interactions within the church were something I chose to be a part of based on a twofold loyalty to God and my dad. I believe in a God that loves and cherishes me and wants the best for me, and that understanding of God comes through my lifelong experiences and love received from my dad. I once prayed for an understanding of God and His love. It felt so abstract until the revelation I was given. God loves me like my dad does, but He knows how to tell me no, even if I cry—when it is not good for me, it is simply not a part of His plan for me. I have lived my life with that understanding ever since, and that reality has helped me to accept each day as it comes. My dad and the church were so integral to my upbringing that it would be hard for me to explain my background and how it impacts my view of the MLK Image without going into at least some basic description of the man I call my dad.

My dad is a strong black man who grew up in a place where things were not always easy for him. He is a brilliant man who somehow figured out how to rise above his situation, take advantage of positive influences and opportunities, and provide a foundation and luxurious existence for his own family. My development of the MLK Image comes from my love and need to understand and respect him while also raising my youngest child in a manner that I believe is in his best interest.

A wise man once said, "Necessity is the mother of invention." Well, I say that love is the mother of understanding, if we allow it to be. Often in life when we hit a divide with people, we stop talking and give up. Too often we fail to resolve the conflict, and we operate with anger and/or unhappiness that destroys our peace. What do you do when what you believe conflicts with the beliefs of not just your parents but basically your whole village? Remember earlier when I mentioned that complicated maneuver? Well here we go. In an effort to keep this book focused, I will not go into much detail outside of the relevant facts. In 2012 the love of my life was born. He was born at less than 24 weeks gestation and at only 1 pound 7 ounces. At his current age of 6, he is considered by many to be a true miracle. I had opened my home to his brothers, who are now ages 25 and 27, when they were in middle school so I had never had the experience of a helpless baby, nor opportunities to bond early with the older two. I am telling you this to explain the motherly instincts that facilitated my internal conflict. I had been raised a certain way, believing a certain thing, and I was now expected to follow through and raise my son with the same direction and goals.

I overthink everything anyway so having a young child put my mind in overdrive, What an awesome privilege and responsibility I had. But, as I considered this, I could not help but struggle as I began to understand the true depth and reality of my responsibility—helping to guide a whole other life from the very beginning to their best and most fulfilling future. I had never had the privilege of being the primary builder of a child's foundation. I began looking at various parents around me and considering what their children had become, and I immediately began to panic. I was hearing and seeing a lot of things that were familiar and seemed right, but as I looked at how their kids had turned out, I could not help but question the process. The plight of kids similar to mine is not so good right now, and there did not appear to be many viable explanations or solutions to increase my son's chances of success.

Past data used to show that children of college-educated individuals who live in a certain type of environment had a higher rate of success. It was a basic equation (Annie E. Casey Foundation, 2011). The belief was, if you get your family out of high-poverty areas and into a "good" school system, then you would be setting your kids up for the same if not greater success than their parents. Studies are now showing that middle- to upper-class, black male boys in two-parent homes are not faring well. Specifically, research is now showing us that the black males born into two-parent homes where the parents are educated and considered on most basic measures to be successful, are not finding success (Badger et al., 2018). As a black person, I have learned over my lifetime that we are masters of denial and misassignment of blame that leaves us paralyzed from growth. But in this scenario, as a single parent attempting this difficult task, I could not afford the traditional blinders because my son is depending on me to figure it out as best I can to provide him with better odds. Then, the questions for me became why is the struggle increasing, and what can I do about it?

This realization of my responsibility began an uncomfortable sequence of debates with my dad in an attempt to reconcile my desire to raise my son based on the things I believe while maintaining myself within the family world of church. Through this series of conversations with not only my dad, but other respected individuals that I have encountered mainly within the church family, I have come to understand the thinking that divides us: the MLK Image. It is my hope that others can find the common ground and understanding that my dad and I continue to work through on our journey.

Before I continue, I feel the need to pause and remind you that my youngest son is still only six at this point in time. I do not neglect the lessons learned while attempting to guide his brothers, but my understanding of the MLK Image did not become a reality until well into their adulthood, and my influence in their lives has now taken on a different role. Therefore, anything I did during their upbringing was subconscious or accidental at best, and any of the knowledge I have gained applied now may have a different impact because of their age. With each of them, I have learned, and I still continue to seek understanding as I guide the youngest. The difference is that now, I am consciously aware that I need to change my behavior during the formative years of his life. This challenges me because I still have many more years to go before I see how my efforts fair as he grows into a man.

Introduction

T HE MLK IMAGE IS A CONCEPTUAL IMAGE OF THE BLACK MAN that draws a deep line in the sand between acceptance and nonacceptance. In the post–civil rights period, the clean-cut, well-spoken image of Dr. King was solidified as the accepted and appropriate standard of what society expects in both the behavior and physical characteristics of an upstanding black man. This is the expectation for the black male that almost every group holds, including the older black generation. It is the most strict and rigid parameters for any group within society and is one of the factors that has made success difficult for the black man as a whole because it provides such a narrow road leading to acceptance. These expectations emanated from various places but mostly derived from society's view of safety: Nonblack men feel safe when encountering the black male who exhibits the MLK Image, and for black males, relaying this image keeps them safe.

For the sake of this writing and because of my own family makeup, my focus is often on the black male; however, there is a parallel understanding of behavior within black females attributed to the MLK Image or, as I refer to it, the Coretta Image, representing the expected behavior and image of the black female. The Coretta Image has impacted the black female to the same degree as it has the male. For example, blacks now have the greatest level of educational disparity between males and females with females representing over 70% of master's degrees for blacks and 66% of doctorate degrees for the race (National Center for Education Statistics, 2016). It is not my stance that this minimizes the struggles that the black female has felt because, in spite of the disparity between males and females, blacks as a whole still show a concerning lack of academic achievement compared to their white and Asian counterparts. My argument is that these struggles have not crippled the black female to the same degree as they have the black male. The rules of acceptance are not as strict for the black female, allowing them more flexibility in individuality while still maintaining the ability to find success in mainstream society. As a whole, black females are still achieving in spite of the hardships and restrictions. Black males, however, have encountered more difficulties.

Regardless of gender, society's lack of understanding and acceptance of blacks' individual choices and preferences continue to define what is right and wrong based on the MLK Image. This misconception has defined a growing number of blacks as outcasts and sometimes dangers to society. This nonacceptance has grown and in some places it is to a level of criminalizing black males strictly based on their physical deviation from this standard, regardless of guilt or innocence. Some individuals base their fear strictly on stereotypes of visual representation. Without a word being spoken or an action taken, black males who do not conform to the MLK Image are often deemed dangerous. Even when proven innocent by the courts, the assumption of danger and wrongdoing is still there. A growing number within society justify these assumptions based on their fears because these black males physically deviate from the "norm." This is, again, in spite of the establishment of innocence. When found guilty, punishments rendered are often more extreme than what is given to whites who commit the same crimes. Other blacks, especially older and those of the conformist mind, justify wrong actions toward black males with statements placing the blame on the victim for how they look, much like that of a rape victim blamed for their clothing choices. I have personally witnessed this dynamic over and over, and when asked why they lack empathy for the person, they say that the person should have known better, shouldn't have looked or dressed the way they did, which has no real basis on actual wrongdoing or guilt. Although black and white issues still exist, what I am pointing out in this dynamic is a bias that has crossed color lines. This type of discriminatory practice based on image comes just as often from blacks, especially older, and those who have conformed to the MLK Image. In the past even I have been guilty of this practice as well. I recall locking my doors in certain places or avoiding certain people strictly based on image. I admit to stereotyping people's abilities based on their outer appearance, but I have now committed to letting go of those stereotypes in favor of learning who people are as individuals.

The MLK Image

The image of what an upstanding, nonthreatening black male looks and acts like mirrors that of the white gentleman. Society views clean-cut, well-spoken, suit-and-tie-wearing gentlemen as less physically dangerous than others who may be more casual in their appearance and demeanor. The nonthreatening image represents civilized behavior in the eyes of society. For blacks, it also became a symbolic portrayal, showing others that you had made it to the more peaceful and cultured side of living.

These beliefs related to a person's acceptable appearance and behavior began with the adoption of European dress culture and the English language by slaves both before and after freedom. Replication of the English language by slaves, since the use of their native tongues was forbidden, resulted in the development of a variation of the language that later became labeled in a negative manner, just like variations in dress and appearance. The English spoken by slaves later gained the description of being "slang," eventually developing into what is now called Ebonics. The line in the sand quickly became a canyon, dividing the good civilized blacks from the unruly dangerous ones based on how they looked and spoke. An even deeper divide was created early on between those blacks who were fortunate enough to have been exposed to education from those who were uneducated, especially in the ability to "speak proper English." Over time, this access to education has become an increasingly key factor in the divide. As these dynamics have manifested, the lack of acceptance for individuals who do not follow the path and portray the acceptable image has grown even greater.

Although the clean-cut image of the white gentleman did not originate and was not necessarily chosen by blacks for reasons of true preference, it was quickly adopted by the culture as acceptable and right. Over time, society continued to apply negative judgments to those who did not conform. These judgments were not just applied by whites but also by those blacks who had adopted the traditions and culture. Books such as *Uncle Tom's Cabin* draw attention to these early divisions, showing how both whites and blacks facilitated these early divides. Terms such as *sellout* and other derogatory notations were applied by blacks to other blacks who "looked and spoke white." In the other direction, labels such as *ghetto, thug,* and *criminal* were applied to those who did not meet the criteria of the mold, with the advantage in the power struggle going to those more closely adhering to the comforts of white society. "Civilized blacks" had begun to join forces with whites in the ridicule and criminalizing of other blacks who did not fit the mold, and the division within the race increased.

Development and Early Stages of the MLK Image

AS A GROUP WITH FREEDOMS AND RIGHTS, MANY BLACK families currently operate with patriarchs and/or matriarchs who are three to five generations from literal slavery. Please pause a second and let that sink in, allowing yourself to understand the true relationship of time. Let me put that into perspective: That means that a person my age (44) could realistically have a grandparent who was raised by the child of a former slave. The beliefs, fears, and experiences of individuals who actually experienced slavery are directly and easily linked to the belief system that we are exposing our children to today based on generational teachings.

Many of the cultural teachings within the black community stem from the overwhelming focus on safety that began during slavery. The mental and physical abuses endured by slaves required the development of a mentality that assisted them in maintaining their lives. Slaves who were found to be insubordinate or defiant were punished in public as an example to deter others' behavior. Public whippings were a regular part of plantation life, with each instance being an event for all to watch. As blacks gained freedom, they were assaulted and hanged without trial or any establishment of guilt. Although I mention these few methods, there were others that were even more inhumane, both physically and emotionally.

These were lessons that no slave, freed man, mother, or father wanted to learn or have their child(ren) learn. Over time, black parents thought that if their rules and punishments were extreme enough, it would deter their sons or daughters from having to endure the master's or white man's harsh and inhumane treatment. Black parents started to believe this type of strict expectation and treatment would create a fear of the parent that was strong enough to deter unacceptable behavior within all environments, especially in public. Ideally, young people would toe the line in fear of what would happen to them at the hands of their parents rather than become victim to the potentially deadly consequences. Although this thinking draws in a large portion of black parents, they will not freely admit to it, but I believe this is true because I've heard black parents say it and I've seen them (and me) do it. This dynamic explains the reputation that black parents have gained over the years of handing out severe or extreme physical punishments. Although some may debate the existence of this dynamic or its cause, it is a topic that we need to examine deeper so that we all can learn and growth.

The Impact of Christianity and the Black Church

Along with the physical fear tactics utilized during slavery, slaves endured psychological and emotional abuse that perpetrated the adoption of the acceptable image of the black man. Christianity was introduced to slaves for both genuine and ingenuine purposes. There were those who introduced the teachings as a means of exposing blacks to salvation and the benefits that they believed Christianity offered, while others introduced Christianity for the purpose of control. Books such as *How to Make a Negro Christian* were guides for slave owners that would assist them in making their slaves more submissive and easier to control by converting them to Christianity. This was a very easy and successful process during this time. An honest review of the history of the race clearly exposes injustices committed toward blacks that have given some black people, both in history and our current day, a justifiably greater appreciation of the Christian promises of a euphoric afterlife that comes with death over the experiences of their everyday living. The dynamics related to the early adoption of Christianity by the black race can take up a whole book, but for our purposes, the early adoption of white culture that Christianity facilitated created a foundational home that established these beliefs and practices as fundamentally right for generations of blacks to come. This paved the groundwork for the MLK Image.

A brief review of the history of the black church shows that during early plantation days as Christianity spread, certain black men were encouraged to be teachers to the others in the spread of Christian beliefs. These individuals were chosen because they were persuasive among the rest of the slaves, and they were often treated in a superior manner for their role in the assimilation of slaves into the Christian faith. Although still slaves, it was obvious in the accommodations, dress, and rations afforded these men that these teachers of the Bible were different. More importantly, they carried a different level of respect both from the master and other slaves. They often served as middle men between the master and other slaves, both helping to improve the conditions for their fellow slaves as well as helping the master maintain the status quo. While controversial in understanding, we cannot deny the documented existence of these individuals during this time. The leadership role of these individuals who were highly respected by the others, along with the respect given to religion, created a customary respect toward leaders within the black church that has maintained throughout the history and growth of the race and faith. This ongoing reverence set the foundation for the success later seen by Dr. King in gaining the respect and admiration of other blacks through his work. This is what made it possible for his voice to even be heard over others expressing similar complaints and concerns, a venue with a regular captive audience that was seeking change.

The early adoption and imitation of white customs and practices within black religion continued even after slaves became free. Although blacks added their own flare to the customary dressy religious attire, the focus on wearing your very best, especially when attending church, became a central characteristic, expectation, and theme within the black church. The continued adherence to these beliefs and practices furthered the feelings of trust toward upstanding black men who carried themselves based on this standard. It also set the groundwork for the replication of this image that we later see in the desire to imitate Dr. King both in his life and work as a pastor and a leader. His maintenance of a safe and respectable image and the resulting trust and respect it produced from whites sealed the beliefs and understanding of an entire generation that the image portrayed was a critical element if one was to find success. On the flip side, it also created a greater void of disapproval and rejection for those who did not seek and portray this image, almost deeming these individuals an embarrassment to those who had "seen the light" and conformed to a "more civilized way of being." The literal interpretation of the Bible and strict expectation of adherence to the values and beliefs taught within the church became the beginning and end in terms of what good black people did and did not do. Those within the church that followed the path have traditionally gained an overall acceptance in exchange for their conformity. Those outside have traditionally been looked down upon and labelled "sinners"—a religious term referring to those perceived to be outside of the rules and desired direction of God. This foundational connection of nonconformity with the "sinner" label further deepened the divide.

Physical expressions, such as tattoos, hairstyles, and personal choices including the consumption of alcohol, sexual behavior, or even dancing, began to represent sin on a level where very little difference was made in the treatment between these individuals and those who had actually committed crimes. Some may debate this opinion, but many of those who are older that conform to the MLK Image literally lack the ability to identify the difference between those expressing their individuality in ways that may be deemed religiously unacceptable and those who are in fact criminals. Even with a significant amount of interaction, many people still may not be able to tell the difference. Although I see a change occurring in this area and a wider level of acceptance beginning to exist, the negative impact continues as well as many of the judgments that facilitated the problem in the first place. I believe that this has become the foundation for the divide that we see between generations that has resulted in the stagnation of the race.

Parents, especially of black males, began seeing their own children as potential criminals that would have to endure the punishments of society. They panicked, just as I did when I began considering the overwhelming responsibility of raising my own son. As a Christian parent, what if my child turns out to be one of those that "fall by the wayside in sin"? How will our family be viewed, and what will I/we do? I cannot just allow them to go to hell and do nothing. I have to try something. An even deeper fear that black parents have is the ultimate fear for their children's actual lives based on what has been taught and experienced in the past—physical harm or even death. What decent parent can realistically look at the potential dangers that their child faces within this world without trying to shield them as best as they can? Earlier, in the Preface, I mentioned that church and family are one in the same for me and my family, but this is not a dynamic seen within my family exclusively. For generations of blacks, the church and its teachings have served as the backbone and moral foundation of the family and community. These desires for safety and the powerful expectations of the church "morally" became the guiding force in many black families' decision making.

During the civil rights era, the church was just the place to reach and maximize opportunities of unity, planning, and encouragement to fuel a movement of such a great magnitude. The success of the movement took a collective effort, and the black church was just the entity to make that happen among blacks. In the post–civil rights era, the image established by Dr. King was maintained as the goal and has been duplicated by pastors, working professionals, and various other blacks, especially the older generation. These expectations spilled over and are strongly linked with acceptance and success in society. This became not just the expectation of those inside but also outside the church as well. The MLK Image carried a great deal of pressure for many of us growing up in the black church, but as each generation has become more and more removed from some of the early purposes of the church, the expectations of those within carried less and less merit.

As mentioned, the impact that the role of the civil rights movement had on the power of the church within the black community was significant, and the separation of the church from this role represented a point of decline. In its current state, the black church has now lost all but a small portion of its political purpose. These fights are left to entities such as the National Association for the Advancement of Colored People (NAACP) and the various other groups and governmental departments purposed for issues of equality. This removed the fight from the everyday black person and made it more of an institutionalized process. The unforeseen outcome of this was a removal from a firsthand understanding and experience for the next generation of children of how these elements of family, country, and religion had fueled the progress of many of our predecessors and their successes of the past. The connection between the moral fight for civil equality and the church was lost, changing the role of the church within both the family as well as the community. My generation may have witnessed some of these fights, heard about them through the hero stories of our parents or grandparents, or even fought them ourselves due to injustices we encountered, but until recent events of the past few years, many of these struggles for the suburban black had all but become taboo. Although issues still ensued, they became few and further between, and with a number of institutions in place to oversee and continue the fight, many people moved on to a more comfortable and relaxed way of living that was influenced very little by the elements of the past.

Post-Slavery

AFTER SLAVERY, BLACKS FOUND OPPORTUNITIES AND WORK in a variety of different places. The depth of racism within the country forced black men and families to find opportunities where they could, seeking the highest level of stability and security they could find. Black males found work in factories and other skill-based professions that afforded them a respectable wage. This allowed many black families the opportunity to own property and other tangible items. One of the most important opportunities that this created, however, was education and opportunities for the children of this early and growing number of financially stable blacks.

Although this early generation of individuals was often uneducated, they knew the value of education and the value of conforming to how society expected them to be and act. I think of my great-grandfather when I consider this group on my father's side, and my grandfather on my mother's side. These men held roles as grandfather/father along with their societally defined role as providers. For many reasons, there has been an intertwining of parenting roles with grandparents within the black community. I will discuss more about this later, but within my family, my great-grandfather was more like my grandfather on my father's side because his role in my father's life was more like a father versus a grandfather, which he actually was. He was the individual who taught my dad the value of hard work through showing him how to work. On a daily basis, he showed my dad how to provide for his family through his example. By no means and under any standards was he considered rich, but he was considered stable, and during that time, hard-working blacks could not and did not ask for much more.

As time went on, the children of this hard-working generation became adults and carried on the traditions of hard work and conformity that they witnessed and learned. These lessons were key elements to success, at least in the minds of many blacks. These individuals, my father's generation, had looked poverty in the face and found stability through hard work and the example set by their parents. These individuals often contributed to the growth of their family through their own hard work and financial contribution. Some had experienced segregated schools and the impacts of Jim Crow racism within this country and still managed to find a respectable place within society. Working hard and overcoming obstacles by using wisdom and knowing how to carry themselves, along with education, was their path toward success. This generation, my dad's generation, surpassed their parents financially to find even greater stability. The issue is that the generation of young people under their care did not seem to respect or understand the work it took to allow them their comforts. The parents of this group had/have no idea how to teach them the simple value of hard work outside of turning their backs on them and allowing them to struggle and fall. This is coupled with an even deeper fear that this generation somehow lacks respect for the dangers in this world that still seem to reflect the difference between life and death at times. Parents base their messages and solutions on conformity to ensure safety and security while the next generation focuses on individuality—a natural conflict of direction.

The Impact of the Civil Rights Era

The civil rights era served as a critical time for blacks, especially the older generation. This is a time in history that represents a huge move for black culture in terms of gaining respect and perceived equality and safety. Prior to this time, blacks struggled time and again for basic human rights. Before this point, blacks had seen very little growth or success in the pursuit of equality with very little direction or support for making it better.

During this time, the work of Dr. Martin Luther King Jr., although not accomplished alone, elevated him among other blacks as the quintessential image of a successful black man and person. He stood up to white men and gained their respect while helping to move the race into what other blacks felt was a better existence. His nonviolent, well-spoken, clean-cut image was already seen by mainstream white society as ideal. His success in gaining whites' respect elevated this image even more, helping it to become the target image for other blacks making strides toward gaining that same respect. This manifested in the replication of his dress, speech, and behavior, which was especially true within the black church—a critical center within the black family and community.

For a generation of blacks who survived the civil rights era and found success, the teachings and MLK Image that they followed to gain their place in the world continued to be the message delivered to their children in spite of the reduced risks of safety and increased financial stability found with the movement's successes. Many black parents continued to teach "survival" messages although survival became less and less of a concern, especially for blacks who migrated to suburban areas. Ironically, parents' hard work to provide a better life for their kids has sheltered their kids from ever really knowing or understanding what it means to not have their basic needs met. Later I will take a look at how these factors impact development and motivation.

The Impact of Suburban Migration

As blacks migrated into the suburbs, the divide between the haves and have-nots within the black race continued to grow following a strict line based on conformity to white standards and expectations—the MLK Image. These standards also began to include educational attainment, with an increased number of blacks finding success in fields and at levels rarely seen previously. These individuals grew up in homes where they often knew poverty and experienced the value of hard work firsthand through the examples set by their parents and grandparents. My dad and his generation exemplifies this group. These individuals were often told the value of education and encouraged to pursue it although their parents were not educated. More importantly, they were shown the value of hard work through their caregivers' efforts to meet the family's basic needs, and were often required to assist in those efforts by working themselves. The value of hard work was a daily reality within their formative years, and the benefits of conformity paid off. The results of education and hard work became a reality in their adulthood as they saw the gains and benefits of their efforts. Their hard work paid off and individuals within this group were often able to give their families a life absent the struggles that they themselves experienced in the past. Maintaining the successful MLK Image was preached to their children along with the importance of acquiring an education, and these things were naturally an expected path. Again, it seemed to be a very basic and simple equation for success.

The embracing of white customs and traditions by slaves and early freed men began as a passive means to lessen the negative treatment. It was believed that by blending in and presenting themselves in a more civilized and cultured manner, they would not draw negative attention from whites, but rather find favor with them. In time, the practice of duplicating white customs and traditions became associated with opportunities for success and acceptance within society. The idea of staying below the radar, sticking to the mold, and portraying an image of safety has become a foundational pillar throughout many generations of black homes, and also an early and ongoing symbol of status for those with the ability and desire to conform. This path to success was relayed to the children of these "crossover" blacks who had found their way from poverty to success, typically through the attainment of education. But their children have not valued or been able to follow the path.

The children of these individuals have often seen very little struggle in contrast to their parents. Worries such as basic needs and safety rarely cross their minds. These families may not be rich, but very often the children have never known what it feels like to go without their basic needs being met. Many of them rarely know what it feels like to hear no. They do not see the value of the path that their parents desire them to take and view it as an effort to control them, thus facilitating a deeper level of disconnect. A growing number of children from this generation express a desire to follow their own path and openly rebel against their parents' teaching, which leaves their parents baffled at what they feel is a lack of desire for security and stability. Why does this obvious disconnect in thinking exist?

The Psychology of the
MLK Image

THE SHEER NATURE OF THE FORMATIVE YEARS CREATES A combative relationship where young people strive for independence from their parents. This is a dynamic understood within the field of psychology as a normal part of development, and seen across races and ethnic groups. This desire for independence and autonomy along with the MLK Image creates the perfect storm of division within the black race. The young say the old are narrow-minded and set in their ways. The old say the young lack respect, discipline, and commitment. The frequency at which either side sits down to develop a mutual understanding has been virtually lost, and the impact is a literal language gap of understanding between the two. Fathers openly express disappointment in their sons, and sons defiantly fight for their honor and place in this world. They share very little in terms of understanding each other but rather relate in their common frustration.

This internal ethnic and racial battle has resulted in the stagnation we currently see within the black community: For the first time in a while, children will not exceed the achievement and financial attainment of their parents. Why has this generation struggled to bridge the divide and move forward in the same ways of those in the past? The answer, I believe, lies in understanding the expectations placed on black males throughout their life and the box that they must force themselves to stay within to be accepted.

Why Are We Stuck?

Although the race has evolved since the dismantling of slavery, many people have retained slavery's survival mentality. Because of this basic life or death mentality about daily survival, especially for the black male, the focus has been on conformity rather than on individuality. Parents have emphasized lessons of survival in an effort to preserve their children's lives based on the long-standing fears instilled throughout slavery and the early Jim Crow existence in this country. Many of these fears continue to be a reality, especially in low-income areas and inner cities. Many black parents continue to utilize these teachings in an effort to preserve their children's lives, teaching them to act and behave a certain way to stay off the radar. This avoidance of danger was, and has remained, the foundational justification for the teaching.

Let me take this a step further for a deeper understanding. When I was younger, even as a black female, I was taught rules related to being pulled over, or how I was to interact with law enforcement, to ensure that nothing I did during a traffic stop resulted in a miscommunication that could put me in a dangerous situation. I, in turn, taught these same rules to my older sons, each as they began to venture out into the community as they got older. Just like my parents, I taught these rules almost as a classroom lesson before both of them obtained their licenses. I did this for the same purpose as those before me—helping to ensure their safety. Anyone with access to the news is aware of the decades-long accusations of police brutality toward blacks. As other blacks read and watch what happens, it creates a natural fear for your own children. People begin to see their own children, or even themselves, at risk of these types of injustices whether the experiences are a reality within their community or not. This type of empathetic fear or projection occurs even if the situation happens in a high-poverty area or inner city and the empathizer lives in an affluent suburb. The result is an entire race of people with the same fears in spite of their varying circumstances.

Over time, these teachings have grown to include beliefs related to the perceived image of a person and how it impacts opportunities for success within society. For blacks to survive mainstream corporate society, they were taught that they have to look safe to others within the environment, specifically whites—the belief being that an image of safety would relay and produce feelings of safety, giving the person a better opportunity for success. These beliefs, keep in mind, had very little to do with a person's actual qualifications. The key was a visual representation of safety.

Although bad things have happened, and continue to, the likelihood of being hurt or killed while living in a suburban area is significantly less than that of an individual living in the inner city. With such different circumstances, why have blacks overall as a race continued to adopt and give priority to the same concerns in spite of the varying conditions? Although some variables are outside of our control, the safety and elevated education quality offered within most suburban environments, as well as the decreased crime, should lead those blacks who are within that environment to change their priorities and move safety out of the number one spot—their kids certainly have. This battle, however, challenges the older generation's belief system to the very core of where many of them exist.

I realized that even when confronted with the reality involved in this type of conformist teaching and thinking, many of the older generation still fight to justify their beliefs based on what they feel is "just doing what it takes to get a chance and make it" or more formally a pragmatic attitude toward life. Although I do not disagree with this understanding of why people conform, this type of thinking lacks the ability to grow and transcend or true equality. This thinking simply accepts the injustice as it is, conforming to it even though it represents judgment and treatment that is not equal nor fair. For example, in our current society, hairstyles are a physical variable that many feel define them visually or express their individuality. For blacks, expression of individuality through hair can often be limited, especially for black males.

The Freedom in Hair

In 2019, for a white female, just about any hairstyle outside of some heavy metal looks would likely be acceptable within the workplace. For a white male, we have also reached a day where this is true depending on the profession. There are some careers where white men still do not traditionally have long hair, but to see a white male with hair of any length, style, or texture really would not be a concern for many.

Black females have fought for their rights to wear more natural styles within the workplace, but discrimination in hiring and other workplace infractions have often been cited when a black woman chooses a nonstraightened or "unkempt" look. For example, I was taught from childhood that I needed to maintain my hair in a fashion that fits the expectations of society for a black female. In other words, no big afros, no locs, and maintaining what society accepts as a "professional look" was what I was taught and what was expected. In 2016 when I decided to adopt a new look and loc my hair, I was met with a great deal of criticism and negative feedback. I went through a very gradual transition to avoid any extreme changes, and by the time I made my full transition, my hair was long enough to be styled in a manner that I felt was acceptable for work. I was very cautious to not draw a great deal of attention to what I was doing to maintain the feelings of safety that my look needed to represent within my profession as a school administrator. Even though it may seem like a lot, more than two years just to transition into a new hairstyle, I step back and have to be grateful that I could even do it and still maintain my job because others have not been so fortunate.

For a black male, these types of changes and individual options simply are not acceptable. Although recently black males are exploring more hairstyle options, the majority of black male professionals still maintain, and are silently and vocally expected to maintain, the same clean-cut MLK Image of the past. This expectation is not seen as optional but rather something that black males coming up in this world who desire success must do. At least this is what the majority of the older generation still believe. Although there are some benefits to this teaching, maintaining this mentality as the culture has assimilated is now creating a negative impact.

Mommy and Daddy Issues

The MLK Image has created a void in parenting that deters the black male's individual social and emotional development. I do not mean this as a disrespectful statement, but rather one that brings a reality or light to what I feel is part of the issue. No decent parent intends to harm their child—I believe this to be foundationally true. No one wants to fail in life—I also believe this to be foundationally true. I also believe, however, that blacks do not consciously know or understand how the generational impacts of the abuses endured skew our ability to see the beautiful forest that exists beyond the tree that blindingly stands in front of us: fear.

For reasons both valid and invalid, black parents continue to focus on safety and fail to see that individuals need to portray themselves and conduct themselves in a manner that recognizes their individual preferences and strengths. I am not implying that we need to embrace individuality to a degree of embracing vulgarities or things of that nature. What I advocate for is that everyone, even black males, should have the freedom to make their own personal choices within the same range of acceptance. I go back to the varying acceptance seen in things such as hairstyles among different types of individuals. Using my earlier example of hair length, if six to eight inches of hair is okay for a white male, then it should be acceptable for a black male as well.

The ongoing existence of these types of biases among the expectations of different groups makes the road to success for the black male more of an uphill climb than what others experience. This is on top of the already difficult societal stereotypes and struggles that have been long-standing hurdles. Although there are some people who have found success, this battle is very difficult and often lacking in adequate and appropriate support. Negative messages often resonate not just from society but also from within the community and home. Black parents raise their children to fit a preexisting mold—the MLK Image. This often neglects the child's individual characteristics, preferences, and strengths. Currently, the rearing of black males successfully has evaded even the best parents. I argue that this is because the needs of our young people, especially our black males, have changed over time, yet our methods and expectations have remained the same.

Psychology 101

To understand this void, I would like to present a quick psychology lesson to provide some basic background knowledge. One of the foremost authorities in understanding development and motivation, Abraham Maslow, developed a theory called Maslow's hierarchy of needs. This theory has stood the test of time and in my opinion allows us to better understand the dynamics mentioned previously. When we look at Maslow's hierarchy of needs, Maslow is basically providing a visual understanding of how the various conditions that we exist within impact how we grow, learn, and develop. The diagram that follows shows how the foundation of our growth begins with our basic stability in having food, water, and shelter and meeting other required or basic needs of life.

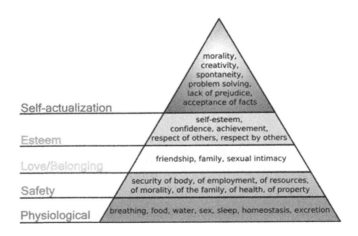

Based on this theory, when we feel stability and certainty that those basic needs are being met, we can then move our focus up to other things. The next level of focus, based on Maslow's triangle, is on safety. For the older generation of black people, although they experience love, friendship, and family, their foundation and focus has been on the maintenance of their safety and physiological needs. There needs to be an understanding that movement from one level to the next within the steps of Maslow's triangle, although fluid at times, requires stability in the lower levels to continue moving upward and maintain at higher levels. That is a complicated concept so I will take it a step further. If we equate the various levels within the triangle to housing, one level represents where we live, while the others, typically one step above or below, are places we visit. The frequency of our visits within those other levels may vary, but our focus and priority always returns to where we live. Having a family and providing for a family does not mean you live at the love and belonging level, it just means you have a positive impact on the stability of those that love and belong to you. I pose that many older blacks have transcended the safety level in the stability that they have found, but in mind and emotion. This crossover generation has continued to live in the mind-set of fear, safety, and security. The divide occurs because they have provided for a higher reality for their children who have often never experienced many of their parents' worries. On the flip side, the parents lack the experiences to know how to teach and train their children to work hard outside of how they themselves learned. Be reminded that during their formative years, many within this crossover generation learned by having to work for their daily meals and to help their family maintain a roof over their heads.

I pause here and revisit my earlier understanding of just how closely the impact of slavery and the philosophies related to safety are embedded in the current rearing of black children. Although the older generation of blacks may have grown up during a time of limited stability in the areas of physiology and safety, their hard work has often allowed their children to begin life at a level of love/belonging and esteem with very little thought or concern for the lower levels.

In a discussion with my dad, I pointed out to him that he would never let me go hungry, homeless, or be harmed if he could help it. He could not in good faith contest that statement. This literally places me standing on his shoulders in security, allowing me an opportunity to reach a higher level of growth and development similar to many other children of this generation of crossover blacks.

It is not my intention to imply that the younger generation is not required to worry or be responsible for maintaining their basic needs. That is not true of any group, including the children of other races. What I am stating is that suburban blacks of my generation and younger do not carry the ongoing worry about these things as our parents did because they have continued to do a great deal of that worrying for us, while also creating a safety net under us. They have provided a better life for the next generation and have no idea how to guide the next generation toward living that life. In an effort to keep the focus on security and safety, which is what they know and believe in, they encourage the next generation to embrace the same conformity that was forced on them, even though the next generation embraces individuality.

In my conversations with my dad, I posed the question, are we to blame our kids and call them spoiled and ungrateful because we shielded them from struggle? Is it my fault that my dad worked hard to give me a life that did not include hunger, homelessness, or danger? Are we now saying our kids should apologize for our hard work and the gains received from it? Or, should the parents apologize for doing the work that allowed the comforts? All of that is nonsense!

Black Parenting

NSTEAD OF BLAMING OUR CHILDREN FOR NOT UNDERSTANDING the hardships we have shielded them from, I believe it is time for parents to step out of the box and discover more impactful and current ways to teach these vital life lessons of hard work and responsibility. Let me be clear, in the past the ways we learned the lessons that led to the development of responsibility and a good work ethic are not effective ways to teach those things to most of our kids today because most of our kids have not faced the same circumstances that previous generations faced. When people are hungry, it is very easy to motivate them to work with a simple promise to feed them. When people do not feel safe, they are very aware and conscious of the things they do to maintain their safety at almost every moment. Many times these are lessons learned without thought or the need for much additional reinforcement. Children that have never gone hungry and never truly felt unsafe are not focused on those things, nor will they ever be until they have an experience that promotes that focus. It does not matter how many stories we tell about walking uphill in the snow both ways to school with a hole in our shoe, they will not effectively get it through secondhand experiences. We have to find a better and more relevant way.

At this point, I can almost hear people screaming that I am being blind and naive to the realities of society by not owning the dangers that continue to exist. I am not blind to the continued struggles facing our world today, and I acknowledge that many of the same dangers of the past still exist, especially for black males. Five minutes watching the news and it is very clear that we still live in some very troubling times. I see these things and feel the same fears that my parents and grandparents felt regarding raising kids. I also, however, see the declining success rate of our black males and an increase in negative experiences associated with them, and I realize something needs to change.

Our Own Front Porch

When I look at the problems facing the black community in 2020, it is hard for me to see past those facilitated and exaggerated by our own behavior. Before the rope hits the tree and my own start pulling me up, let me explain. We cannot fix what is outside until we address the internal issues, so we may as well put our thick skin on and shine a light on the truth.

Although I have never been a slave in the literal sense, I now realize that I have to make a conscious effort to let go of some of the destructive and limiting generational beliefs, thoughts, and practices that have resulted from it. As a race we have to remember that many of the things that were taught to blacks during slavery were done through abusive practices that were not for the purpose of growth, but rather control and restriction. In time, many people forgot the negative origins and purpose of these teachings, only recognizing the success and comforts that the conformity afforded. Reflecting back on Maslow, there is only so high you can reach while maintaining your focus on safety and security.

The characteristics and description associated with group thinking and group belief systems provides an understanding that mentalities, beliefs, and practices are taught from one generation to the next. With such a significant common event, such as slavery, happening in the lives of one race, it was very easy to conform the race to a common way of thinking and behaving. When we consider the life or death nature of what some of these beliefs and practices represent(ed), it is no surprise that transitioning the race as a whole to a place where individuality is the focus, especially for the endangered black male, has been an elusive task. The sheer nature of group thinking creates an all-against-one mentality toward those who do not conform and those who choose to go against the grain. Blacks have focused on the need to survive and find stability for so long that we struggle to know anything else—blacks are masters of survival mode.

As changes in family socioeconomic status have occurred, and some families now live in safer environments, the focus on safety, security, and conformity continued. This is in contrast to a mind-set promoting individuality. In theory, as the conditions facing black families changed, the focus from conformity to individuality should have transitioned as well. However, it did not.

The Benefits of Conformity

For freed blacks, maintaining safety and becoming stable financially were the primary aims. Accordingly, to bring those goals into fruition, blacks continued to conform to society's expectations, teaching future generations to do the same, and that makes sense. This continued for the next few generations after the Civil War and throughout the civil rights era. For a period of time this focus continued to make sense as a priority for the race. This is especially true as blacks fought for rights and opportunities. I believe that the crossover generation has, however, ushered us into a new existence. Growth has occurred for many black families with some now moving toward abundance, but the focus on survival has never diminished. I pose that the divide that we see today is a manifestation of this continued priority on conformity within our teaching, and a lack of adjustment to priori-tize individuality. The focus has remained on conformity instead of moving forward and breaking out of the expected image. It should be the goal for all to someday feel this freedom without consequence.

The efforts to fight for this equality have been limited and mainly facilitated by a younger, less influential group. At times, this younger group has had to fight the criticisms and resistance of older blacks, along with the judgments and expectations of traditional society. The lack of support from the older generation for breaking free from the expected mold and embracing individuality limits the strength of the fight, and has left blacks continuing to conform to many of the visual expectations and limitations of past generations. Black people in general stand as a house divided on many issues because the older and younger generations do not see from the same lens nor do they have the same focus. Meanwhile, an increasing number of black boys struggle to become men who survive in a productive and healthy manner within this world, mainly because they do not fit the mold and are shown very little tolerance for being themselves.

Depending on your thinking, there are two questions that exist to help determine the next steps if blacks are to effectively address the black male's declining success:

- Why does this generation not see the benefits of conformity, and how do we get them to begin seeing these benefits?
- How do we adjust our thinking to accept individuals' expressions, especially black males, without applying the traditional negative labels and feelings?

As a race, we have mainly placed our focus and efforts on the first option of finding a way to sell conformity. How is that working for us? Earlier I mentioned the fact that black boys born into two-parent, stable homes are not doing well. I mentioned earlier that for the first time in a while, children will not surpass their parents financially. Again I ask, how is that working for us?

I choose the second option.

Solution

I F YOU ARE ACTUALLY LOOKING FOR A STEP-BY-STEP ACTION PLAN in this book, you have completely missed the point of what I have discussed. Individuality is just that, individual. A solution for the crisis facing black males in this country begins with getting to know each and every one of our children to the greatest depth possible, and embracing the qualities and characteristics that we see within them in a positive manner. I think I should state that again because I feel it is important: A solution for the crisis facing black males in this country begins with getting to know each and every one of our children to the greatest depth possible, and embracing the qualities and characteristics that we see within them in a positive manner. This is not just for black males. This is critical for everyone, but black males simply experience it the least.

As parents, we have to force ourselves to identify and somehow embrace these qualities within our children, no matter how different they may be than us. This does not mean that we have to accept and condone all behaviors. We don't. It simply means we need to try to find a way to understand the behaviors and how they relate to our individual child's personality and strengths. Once we understand this, it is the parents' responsibility to then do our best to find a way to direct those behaviors in a positive and productive direction. I believe that every parent should work to identify their child's personality type, strengths, weaknesses, and likes and do the best job they can to facilitate their child's positive growth within that natural path. It is not our job to mold our children to become clones of ourselves or anyone else. It is our job to help them be the very best them that they can become. It is a chess game: They act, you react. You act, they react. Finding the right balance within the interaction keeps life moving forward.

Reframing

The question is, where do we go from here and how do parents begin to discover and understand their child to the degree mentioned previously? How do parents increase the positive impact that they have on their child's overall direction and growth, especially if their child is a black male? In many instances, I feel we truly do know our kids, but there are some things we do not want to accept because we attach a negative feeling or stigma to the behavior. Behaviors that result in labels such as *stubbornness* and *defiance* at an early age are often labeled *perseverance* and *creativity* as one gets older. These tendencies, which later could become strengths, are often discouraged rather than nurtured as positives. There are various behaviors that carry this type of dual understanding that changes over time. Another example would be an individual who is labeled as *chatty* or *inappropriately talkative* at a young age who later finds success as an attorney or public speaker.

Black males are often described as being characteristically aggressive. They are also accused of reckless decision making and behavior. Let us consider this from the opposite or positive direction. What if that aggressiveness is relabeled as being a go-getter with persistence and perseverance? In that same light, what if reckless decision making for black males, being reminded of the small box of tolerance given the group, was actually an early sign of someone who is adventurous and creative? Once again, many of the qualities that receive a negative stigma early on if properly developed could actually become strengths that lead to success later in life. Here is the problem and I am going to call it like I see it: It takes a lot more thought and effort to figure out all the vital elements of who your child is than it does to just keep the course of conformity, plus you have to be aware of the need. No, I am not implying that parents have been lazy. I am also not saying that they have failed to put forth their best effort based on what they knew. I honestly believe that the cross-over generation of parents have had the most difficult job that parents of black children have faced in a long time due to the transition of conditions that have occurred during their charge. What I am saying is they did not have a conscious awareness of the changes that were happening nor did they have a great toolbox of skills and experiences to know how to handle these changes that they were unknowingly living through. Their kids were being raised under completely new circumstances for most black families, and parents were blind to the long-term impact of these new conditions, while still applying the old rules and thinking. How do we embrace the improved conditions of many blacks and still teach the work ethic and responsibility of the past? How do we identify and nurture qualities that we see within our children with a positive understanding rather than destroy them with negative responses to their behaviors? How is this done while also respecting the fundamental need for safety and security within our society? These are the types of questions that I feel we must answer to get over this hump as parents.

Balance

Somewhere between the extremes of restriction and conformity, in contrast to complete freedom, lies a compromising point that black parents and black males need to find. We have established that the ways of the past do not work for a growing number of young people, but we also know that there are dangers and risks that still exist. Where is the balancing point between guiding our children toward a safe and secure existence and helping them to discover and become their very best individual self?

I pose that this balance is different for every group and community and has to be determined based on a truthful and conscientious look at the conditions of the supporting environment. The basic foundations of Maslow's triangle do not change. People need security in areas of basic needs to move forward. When they obtain that security, the balance of priority must shift as well to incorporate the new focus and needs. This balance may exist at one point for a black family that lives in the inner city of St. Louis, Missouri, and be completely different for a family residing in Edwardsville, Illinois. These two cities represent less than a 30-minute difference in location but a world of difference in dynamics. Families that live in these two places, although close in location, do not share the exact same concerns and, therefore, should not raise their kids with the exact same priorities. Is this fair? No. I did not begin this adventure searching for fair. I began this journey seeking a way to increase the chances of success for my son.

I do not like the inequalities seen between environments anymore than the next person, but that does not mean I have to embrace the fears of another person who is in completely different conditions than me to be supportive. I do not have to project these fears as my own and operate within my environment based on these same frustrations and concerns. My job as I grow and gain stability and comfort is to keep moving forward and work to open greater doors of equality and acceptance for a wider group of people. For me to do this, I have to continue to grow and achieve, not remain stagnant.

The only way that we can help others is to get to know them and be a positive influence on their growth to becoming their very best self. We need to promote this not based on how or what we feel they should be, but rather based on what their characteristics, skills, and likes direct them to become. If each of us operate within our daily lives in this way and raise our children in this manner, then our goal becomes personal growth and development, not the replication of someone else's mold and behavior. In my daily life, my job is to live within the opportunities and conditions that I exist, not based on someone else's experiences. When we embrace our own reality with self-honesty, I argue that success is inevitable because we are gauging it on the path and expectations that we have chosen, not what someone else has forced us to take. This acceptance and choice should inherently create our own accountability for our choices as well as successes.

The bottom line is as black families move toward more security, the focus of teaching must adjust to a greater acknowledgment and pursuit of individuality. Equally critical in areas where there is a lack of safety and opportunity for stability, there must be a continuous fight to increase these elements in order to secure a better and more individually focused existence for these families as well. These two areas of focus, security and individuality, must begin to operate in greater harmony for black males to see a better day as a whole. The expectations must adjust to allow everyone to operate and grow on a path that is best for each individual, not in conformity to an unrealistic group norm based in fear.

Conclusion

LTHOUGH I HAVE DIRECTED THIS BOOK TOWARD THE BLACK community because of my original purpose, many of the elements mentioned cross racial boundaries, especially in the solution section. Everyone needs acknowledgment and nurturing of their individual tendencies, strengths, and likes. There are families of all types both excelling and lacking in this area. I target the black male in this writing because of my sons and my current responsibility to guide them in the best way I know. The current situation for black males and their success as a whole also makes me feel that they are the group who needs more assistance. Once we understand the black male's critical needs, we have to acknowledge that this issue is comparable for those who live below the poverty line. I definitely do not want to start digging into that conversation at this point, but the correlation of growth from one level of Maslow's triangle to the next fits closer with the various stages of economic growth than racial lines do currently.

As I have continued to grow in my understanding of the dynamics discussed in this book, I still find myself very frustrated and confused at my next steps. Kids are kids and there is no manual for problem solving every situation related to them. All we can do is put our love and thoughtfulness into our interactions with our children while applying the understanding we have of their needs. I just laughed at myself for even writing something so unrealistic. To think we have this awareness as parents within every situation is definitely a lot to expect. We need to both forgive ourselves as parents right up front and own the impossibility of perfection because parenting can be emotionally exhausting and frustrating. How about we agree to simply do our best to operate within this light, with an understanding that there will always be shortcomings and mistakes.

My hope is to engage a wide variety of individuals in the conversations that this book starts. I fear that my open discussion of a number of vital historical elements behind the MLK Image may create discomfort for some, which may deter their participation. Specifically, I hope that people within the black church as well as whites approach this work with an open mind and heart. There were a number of times during the writing process where I felt uncomfortable. One of the best things I did to alleviate this feeling was to begin talking about it even more. I began opening up the discussion with my parents and other individuals around me. I even found the opportunity to discuss some of my discoveries with my dental hygienist. When I explained to her my why in terms of what caused me to begin down this road, I looked up to see tears in her eyes. The respect and love within my family opened the door to a beautiful opportunity to give credit and proper respect to the generation that paved the way for my individuality. The love that facilitates this type of push for understanding, the love for my dad as well as the love for my son, is the key that opened my mind to understanding. This has to be the foundation for everyone if the goal is to truly open our eyes to our children's needs.

Although I am grateful for the understanding that I have gained, I feel a certain pressure to act now that I know. I have made decisions about school that were based on what I feel is a true assessment of my son's needs at this point in his life. With his teacher's input as well as observation, I am working to identify my youngest's learning style. He is relentless when he wants something and resistant at other times. In other words, he is stubborn, but in allowing him some flexibility in those areas, I have already seen him grow out of many of the negative behaviors and start to exhibit a relentless attitude toward problem solving. He is learning to approach issues from various directions until he finds a solution. Does this require me hearing some whining at times? I wish I had another few pages just to whine myself and tell the stories, but this is not about me. And when we choose to raise kids, we need to start with that understanding. We as parents need to build a bit more resiliency so we can allow our children more flexibility to grow.

Now that your brain has been overloaded and you are trying to sort through what you agree with and what you do not, it is my opinion that the next steps center around discussions and conversations with other people. Remember what I stated earlier: Healthy conversation and debate is what kept my thinking moving forward to come to this point—conversations not just with people who look or act like you, but also with those who are different. This is critical because I believe we must eventually come to a point where we see this beyond race and start owning the impact that our economic biases have on these social dynamics as well.

One of the scariest, yet one of the most important, things I did before I ever approached a publisher with this book was to ask one of my trusted, honest, conservative white friends to read it. Equally nerve-wracking was requesting an honest read from my parents—the forty-plus-year pastor and first lady of a Baptist church. It was not until I got a thumbs up from both that I moved forward. My explanation for this is simple: This book is meant to be a work that unites, not divides.

I pray that this book meets that purpose and serves as a stimulus for healing and reconciliation not just for the black male, but for our broken society as a whole.

Works Cited

Annie E. Casey Foundation. 2011. *Promoting Opportunity for the Next Generation: America's Children, America's Challenge: 2011 KIDS COUNT Data Book, 2011: State Profiles of Child Well-Being*. Baltimore: Author.

Badger, E., Miller, C. C., Pearce, A., and Quealy, K. 2018. "Extensive Data Shows Punishing Reach of Racism for Black Boys." *New York Times*, March 19, 2018. https://www.nytimes.com/interactive/2018/03/19/upshot/race-class-white-and-black-men.html.

National Center for Education Statistics. 2016. "Degrees Conferred by Race and Sex." Retrieved December 3, 2019. https://nces.ed.gov/fastfacts/display.asp?id=72.

Made in the USA
Monee, IL
29 February 2020